Life After The Narcissist

Companion Journal

This journal belongs to:

_____

_____

© Copyright 2025 - All rights reserved.

The content contained within this book may not be reproduced, duplicated or transmitted without direct written permission from the author or the publisher.

Under no circumstances will any blame or legal responsibility be held against the publisher, or author, for any damages, reparation, or monetary loss due to the information contained within this book, either directly or indirectly.

Legal Notice:
This book is copyright protected. It is only for personal use. You cannot amend, distribute, sell, use, quote or paraphrase any part, or the content within this book, without the consent of the author or publisher.

Disclaimer Notice:
Please note the information contained within this document is for educational and entertainment purposes only. All effort has been executed to present accurate, up to date, reliable, complete information. No warranties of any kind are declared or implied. Readers acknowledge that the author is not engaged in the rendering of legal, financial, medical or professional advice. The content within this book has been derived from various sources. Please consult a licensed professional before attempting any techniques outlined in this book.

By reading this document, the reader agrees that under no circumstances is the author responsible for any losses, direct or indirect, that are incurred as a result of the use of the information contained within this document, including, but not limited to, errors, omissions, or inaccuracies.

Cover design by Jennifer Stimson.

A Letter to You

Welcome.

Recovering from narcissistic abuse can feel like learning to breathe again after holding your breath for as long as you can remember. Some days, you'll feel strong and hopeful. Other days, it may feel like you're starting over, and that's completely normal.

This journal was created to walk beside you through these ups and downs, one page, one prompt, one step forward at a time. Inside, you'll find many reflective questions from *Life After The Narcissist*, now expanded with new prompts to help you go even deeper. Each section draws from the eight chapters in the book and is designed to guide you through self-reflection, emotional release, and rediscovery of your true self. You'll watch your thoughts, fears, and breakthroughs take shape on each page, and over time, you'll begin to notice your inner strength shining through in every word you write.

There's no "right" way to use this journal. Some days, you may write paragraphs. Other days, just a few words and that's enough. These pages aren't about perfection; they're about showing up for yourself as your own best friend.

Take your time, breathe deeply, and remember: you are not alone on this journey.

Building A Safe Community

After completing the Life After the Narcissist Companion Journal, if you found support and healing on your journey, I would be deeply grateful if you could leave a review. Your thoughtful feedback, shared after your experience with the journal, can offer comfort and hope to others who are beginning their path to recovery. Even a few sentences about how it helped you can make a powerful difference, helping someone feel less alone and more empowered to start their own healing process.

Thank you for your kindness and for sharing your thoughts.

Chapter 1

Understanding Narcissistic Abuse

When did you first notice something felt 'off' in your relationship? Describe that moment in detail, and honor its importance without minimizing or dismissing it.

Recall a time when you changed your behavior to make someone else feel more comfortable, even though it didn't feel right to you. How did that impact your emotions and thoughts?

_____
_____
_____
_____
_____
_____
_____
_____
_____
_____
_____
_____
_____
_____
_____
_____

Body Check-In

Place your hand on your chest or stomach and take a deep breath. As you think about reclaiming your story, what physical sensation do you notice?
Write one word or a short phrase to capture it.

Recall a moment in your relationship when you felt dismissed, confused, or invisible. What words of kindness and support would you want to hear then to feel seen and valued?

In what ways did the abuse make you doubt yourself?

For example, you second-guessed your memories, hesitated to speak up, or worried that your feelings weren't valid.

How are you learning to trust yourself again now?

What coping strategies did you lean on to survive, such as people-pleasing, overworking, or shutting down?

_____
_____
_____
_____
_____
_____
_____
_____
_____
_____
_____
_____
_____

Which ones helped you, and which ones caused more pain?

_____
_____
_____
_____
_____
_____
_____
_____
_____
_____
_____
_____

What has made it hard for you to leave the relationship, whether due to practical reasons or emotional ties?

_____
_____
_____
_____
_____
_____
_____
_____
_____
_____
_____
_____

How has understanding narcissistic abuse changed the way you view your past or the people involved?

_____
_____
_____
_____
_____
_____
_____
_____
_____
_____
_____
_____

Affirmation

Choose one affirmation that speaks to you, or write your own:

- ☐ I deserve to set boundaries that protect my peace.
- ☐ I am gently learning to trust myself again.
- ☐ I have the right to feel safe, no matter what others may think.

Letter to Your Past Self

Write a letter to the version of yourself before you understood what you know now. What advice, comfort, or encouragement would you offer them to help them through that time?

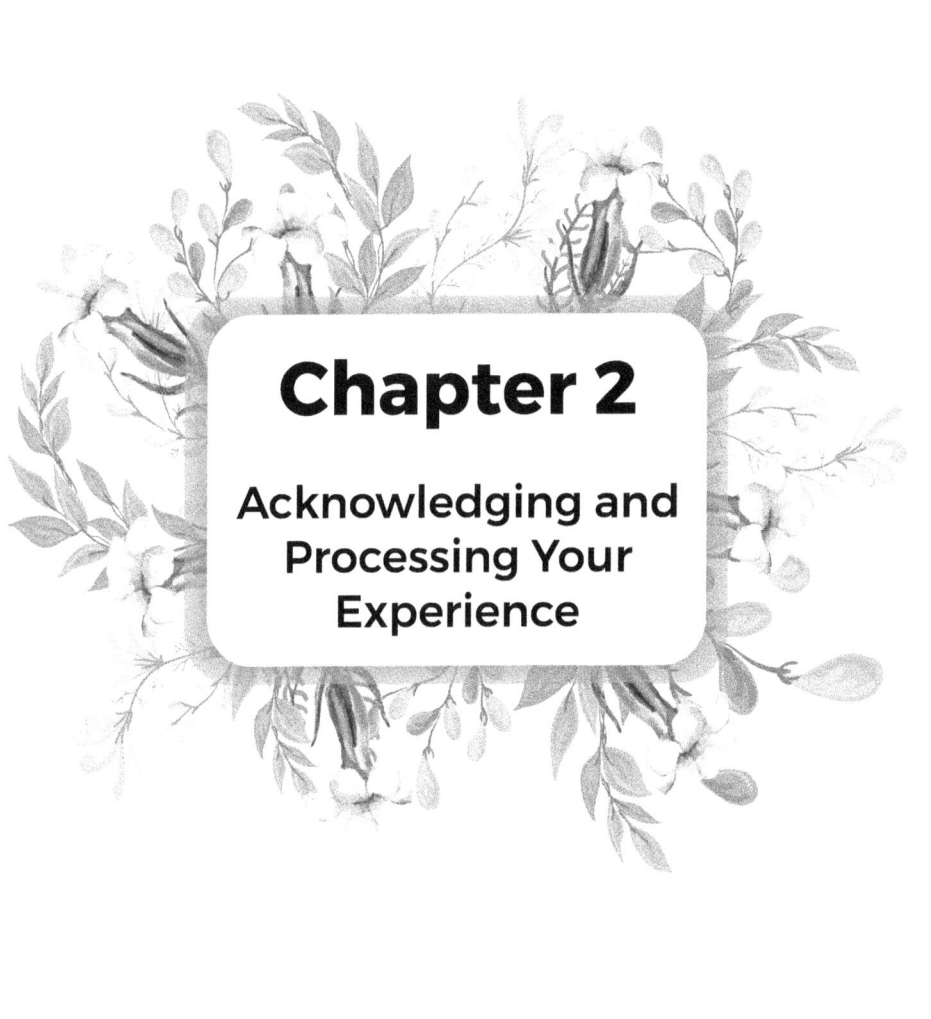

Chapter 2

Acknowledging and Processing Your Experience

After experiencing narcissistic abuse, it's natural to minimize or justify what happened. Can you notice times when you still do this? Begin writing about what truly occurred, and explore how you might start reframing your story to honor your truth and feelings.

Think back to a time when denial helped you get through a difficult moment. What was it that eventually helped you begin to face the truth?

_____
_____
_____
_____
_____
_____
_____
_____
_____
_____
_____

Do you find it difficult to label your experience as "abuse"? What feelings come up when you consider this word?

_____
_____
_____
_____
_____
_____
_____
_____
_____
_____

What losses are you grieving at this moment?
It might be lost time, aspects of your identity, the kind of love you once believed in, or something else meaningful to you.

Have you ever blamed yourself with thoughts like, "I wish I'd seen it sooner" or "I wish I'd acted differently"?
Gently explore these feelings and how you might show compassion to them and yourself.

What habits do you notice that were shaped by the narcissist's influence?

Maybe you keep the TV volume low even when alone, keeping yourself constantly busy, or staying silent to avoid conflict.

Write about the habits you feel ready to start changing now.

_____
_____
_____
_____
_____
_____
_____
_____
_____
_____
_____
_____
_____
_____
_____
_____
_____
_____
_____
_____
_____
_____
_____
_____

Mirror Exercise

Stand before a mirror and say to yourself:
"I did the best I could with the knowledge I had then."
Notice whatever feelings come up, discomfort, resistance, sadness, or calm.
Use this space to reflect on how it feels to accept what's present.

Chapter 3

Laying the Foundations for Healing

Reflect on the small victories you experienced today.
Maybe it was getting out of bed despite how you felt, sending a message you were nervous about, or choosing a calmer response than before.
Write about these moments and how they made you feel.

Choose a practice from Chapter 3 that feels grounding and supportive for you today, something that meets you exactly where you are.

Before You Begin

Which word best describes what you notice?
Body: pain, warmth, tingling
Mind: restless, calm
Breath: fast, slow, shallow, deep

_____
_____
_____
_____
_____
_____
_____
_____

After Your Practice

Reflect on your session. What shifts did you notice in your body, mind, or emotions?

_____
_____
_____
_____
_____
_____
_____

How are you choosing yourself, one decision at a time?
Reflect on a recent moment when you paused, reflected,
or said no, without needing to justify yourself.

_____
_____
_____
_____
_____
_____
_____
_____
_____
_____
_____
_____
_____
_____
_____
_____
_____
_____
_____
_____
_____
_____
_____
_____
_____
_____
_____
_____
_____
_____

Support That Heals

Make a list of the people, places, and rituals that nurture your healing. Who or what helps you feel safe, centered, and seen? Try to do one small action from your list every day.

People

_____
_____
_____
_____
_____
_____
_____

Places

_____
_____
_____
_____
_____
_____
_____

Rituals

_____
_____
_____
_____
_____
_____
_____

What small boundaries can you begin to set today to safeguard your healing?
It might be taking longer to respond, stepping away from difficult conversations, or carving out quiet time without explanation.

_____
_____
_____
_____
_____
_____
_____
_____
_____
_____
_____
_____
_____
_____
_____
_____
_____
_____
_____
_____
_____
_____
_____
_____
_____
_____

Which old patterns have you noticed creeping back in recently, and how did you respond?

Think about a moment today when you showed yourself kindness. What did it look like, and how did it make you feel in your body and mind? Write about that experience.

_____
_____
_____
_____
_____
_____
_____
_____
_____
_____
_____
_____
_____
_____
_____
_____
_____
_____
_____
_____
_____
_____
_____
_____
_____
_____

Visualizing Your Safe Space

Close your eyes and imagine a place where you feel completely safe and relaxed.

What does this space look like?
Who, if anyone, is with you?
What sensations do you notice in your body as you rest in this safe space?
Write about this place with as much detail as you can. Return here in your mind whenever things feel overwhelming.

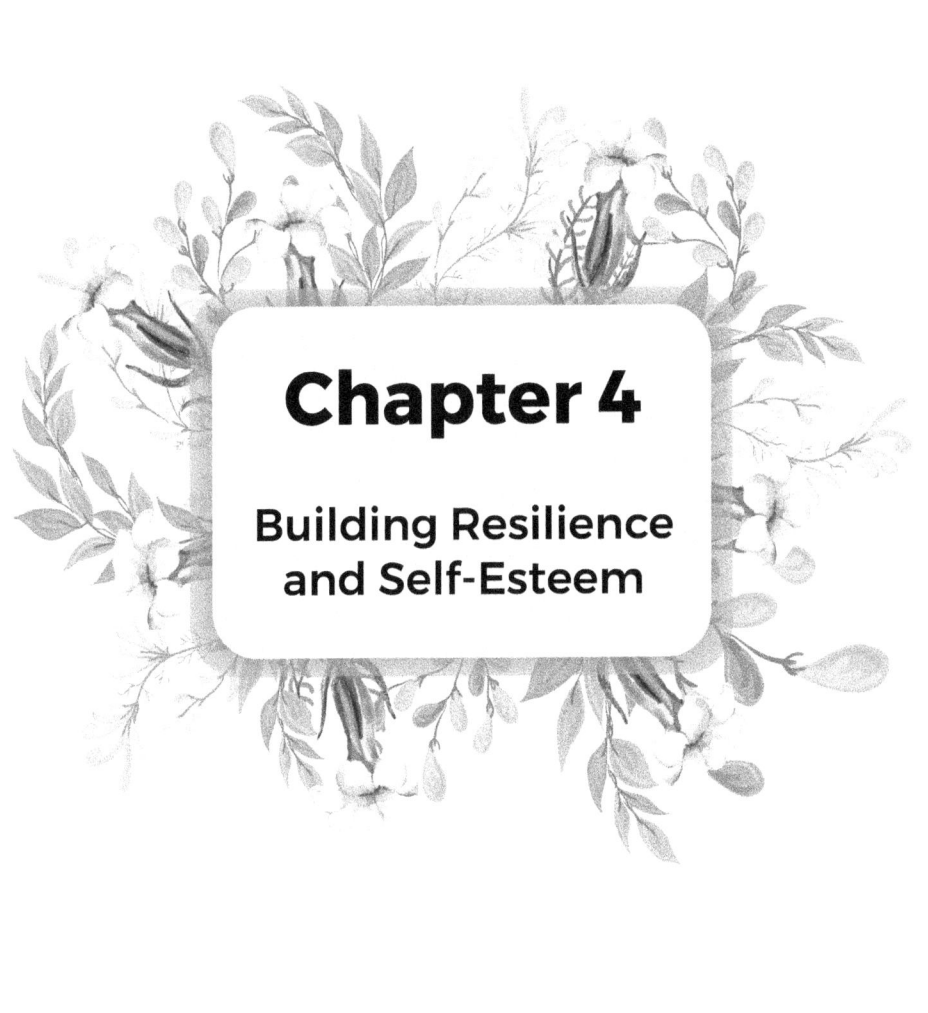

Chapter 4

Building Resilience and Self-Esteem

Identifying Personal Strengths

Skills that helped me survive:
Staying calm, problem-solving, adapting quickly.

_____
_____
_____
_____
_____
_____
_____
_____
_____
_____

My natural abilities:
Reading people, finding humor, making others feel safe.

_____
_____
_____
_____
_____
_____
_____
_____
_____
_____

Qualities others value in me:
Loyalty, empathy, grit, strength.

Challenges I've overcome:
Leaving, starting over, speaking my truth.

Reflection

When did you feel most alive before the narcissistic relationship? Recall what your past self was doing, feeling, believing.
If that memory feels distant, try looking through old photo albums or your camera roll.

_____
_____
_____
_____
_____
_____
_____
_____
_____
_____
_____
_____
_____
_____
_____
_____
_____
_____
_____
_____
_____
_____
_____
_____

What are the things you do without overthinking, when you follow your intuition? Notice what excites or energizes you and write your first thoughts about them.

A Day in the Life: Self-Awareness Inventory

Each evening, take a few minutes to check in with yourself. Use the space below to track your reflections over the next seven days.

Day 1

Three things I handled well today

1._____
2._____
3._____

One moment when I felt confident

_____

_____

One challenge I faced

_____

_____

How I dealt with it

_____

_____

_____

_____

_____

_____

_____

Day 2

Three things I handled well today

1. _____
2. _____
3. _____

One moment when I felt confident

_____
_____

One challenge I faced

_____
_____

How I dealt with it

_____
_____
_____
_____
_____
_____
_____
_____
_____
_____
_____
_____

Day 3

Three things I handled well today

1. _____
2. _____
3. _____

One moment when I felt confident

_____

_____

One challenge I faced

_____

_____

How I dealt with it

_____

_____

_____

_____

_____

_____

_____

_____

_____

_____

_____

Day 4

Three things I handled well today

1. _____
2. _____
3. _____

One moment when I felt confident

_____

_____

One challenge I faced

_____

_____

How I dealt with it

_____
_____
_____
_____
_____
_____
_____
_____
_____
_____
_____

Day 5

Three things I handled well today

1. _____
2. _____
3. _____

One moment when I felt confident

_____
_____

One challenge I faced

_____
_____

How I dealt with it

_____
_____
_____
_____
_____
_____
_____
_____
_____
_____
_____
_____

Day 6

Three things I handled well today

1. _____
2. _____
3. _____

One moment when I felt confident

_____
_____

One challenge I faced

_____
_____

How I dealt with it

_____
_____
_____
_____
_____
_____
_____
_____
_____
_____
_____
_____

Day 7

Three things I handled well today

1. _____
2. _____
3. _____

One moment when I felt confident

_____
_____

One challenge I faced

_____
_____

How I dealt with it

_____
_____
_____
_____
_____
_____
_____
_____
_____
_____

Feedback From Others

Choose one person from your safe list and ask them:

What strengths do you see in me?
When have you seen me at my best?
What do you admire about how I've handled this past year?

Write their answers below.

Now take a moment to reflect:
Did anything they shared challenge a self-critical belief
like "I'm not lovable" or "I'm not enough"?
If so, which beliefs began to shift for you?

_____
_____
_____
_____
_____
_____
_____
_____
_____
_____
_____
_____
_____
_____
_____
_____
_____
_____
_____
_____
_____
_____
_____
_____
_____

Which specific boundary have I struggled to maintain, and what practical step can I take today to reinforce it?

Daily Reflection

There's no right or wrong way to use these prompts. Choose one each day and write whatever feels right to you. Some questions might bring up strong emotions and that's perfectly okay. Take your time, be kind to yourself, and let your words come naturally.

What made me feel strong today?

___
___
___
___
___
___
___
___
___
___
___
___
___
___
___
___
___
___
___
___
___
___

When do I feel most like myself?

What would I say to my younger self?

If I could tell someone exactly how I feel, without consequences, what would I say?

What am I proud of myself for?

What do I want my life to look like one year from now?

When did I last feel truly peaceful?

What does safety feel like to me?

Which parts of myself did I hide during the relationship?

What's one thing I did today that shows I'm moving forward, no matter how small?

What do I need right now that I'm afraid to ask for?

When did I last trust my gut feeling? What happened?

Since starting this healing journey, which old beliefs do I still carry that I'm ready to let go of now?

What would I do differently if I knew no one would judge me?

Moments I'm proud of:
Setting a boundary, trusting my gut, showing up for myself.

Your Story Circle

Following the book's suggestion to build a trusted "story circle," what stories from your life do you feel ready to share? *This might be a moment of strength, vulnerability, or something that helped you survive.*

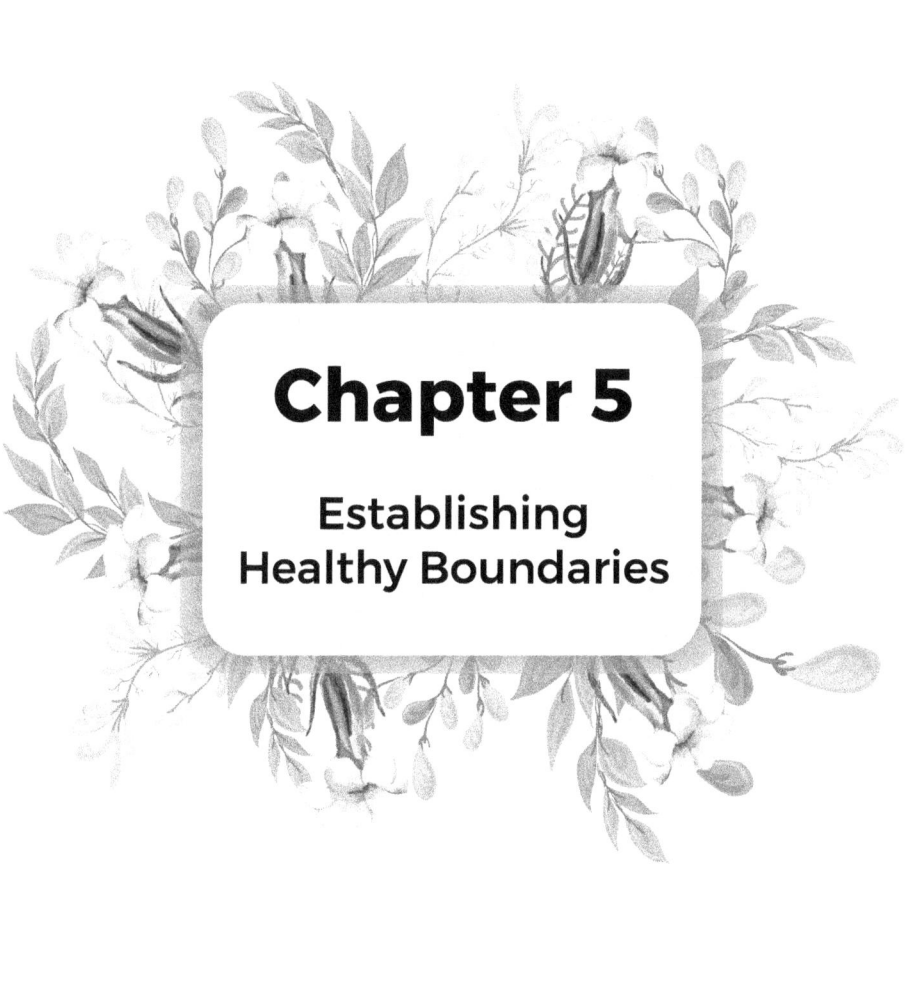

Chapter 5

Establishing Healthy Boundaries

What beliefs about boundaries did you grow up with?
For example, were you taught that saying 'no' is rude or selfish?

Describe how these beliefs affect your ability to set limits now.

Emotional Boundary Inventory

Sometimes emotional boundary violations can be hard to notice because they show up disguised as love, concern, or honesty. Think back to a time when your body signaled that a boundary was being crossed before your mind could explain why.

What sensations did you notice?
Examples: Tightness in the stomach, nausea, heaviness

_____
_____
_____
_____
_____

What did you do in that moment?

_____
_____
_____
_____
_____
_____
_____
_____
_____
_____
_____
_____
_____
_____

How might you respond differently now?

Reflect on these four ways emotional boundaries can be crossed.

Emotional Dumping

When someone shares their struggles intensely without checking if you're available to listen, it can leave you feeling overwhelmed. Think about moments when this has happened to you.

What are some phrases or responses you could use to protect your energy and create space for yourself?

_____
_____
_____
_____
_____
_____
_____
_____
_____
_____
_____
_____
_____
_____
_____
_____
_____
_____
_____
_____
_____
_____

Guilt Manipulation

Sometimes people use guilt to influence your choices, making you feel pressured or responsible.
Reflect on times when you've felt this way.

What compassionate, firm responses can you use to honor your boundaries and reclaim your energy?

Emotional Invalidation

When your feelings are dismissed or minimized, it can leave you doubting yourself.
Recall experiences when this may have happened.

How can you remind yourself of your truth, stand firmly in your feelings, and move forward with confidence?

_____
_____
_____
_____
_____
_____
_____
_____
_____
_____
_____
_____
_____
_____
_____
_____
_____
_____
_____
_____
_____
_____

Forced Intimacy

Sometimes people expect closeness or openness before you're ready. Think about moments when your emotional boundaries have felt rushed or crossed.

What steps can you take to honor your own pace, protect your space, and respect your level of readiness?

_____
_____
_____
_____
_____
_____
_____
_____
_____
_____
_____
_____
_____
_____
_____
_____
_____
_____
_____
_____
_____
_____

Who in your life consistently disrespects your time, interrupts you, shows up late, or makes last-minute changes? Consider clients, coworkers, friends, children, or family. List them below. Then write a response you could use next time to protect your time.

Examples:
"I can't talk right now, but I'll call you at 6."
"I need more notice for schedule changes."
"I'm not available during work hours."

Think back to childhood. What were you taught directly
or indirectly to expect from relationships?

Examples:
"If I'm good, people will love me."
"I have to earn affection."
"Being needed means being loved."

Choose one early message and write it down:

_____
_____
_____
_____

Is it true?

_____

Is it helpful?

_____

What's a more honest, compassionate belief you could hold instead?

_____
_____
_____
_____
_____
_____
_____
_____
_____
_____

Chapter 6

Emotional Well-being

Creative Expression

Write a poem, song lyrics, or free writing that shares a feeling you haven't had the chance to express yet. It could be about something recent or something you've held onto for a long time. Give yourself permission to explore your emotions without judgment.

Visual Art

Use this page to draw, paint, or create simply for the joy of it, without worrying about skill or how it turns out. Let colors and shapes express what words can't.

Identify Your Triggers

What situations today still trigger feelings connected to your experience with the narcissistic relationship?

Tracking these triggers for up to two weeks can reveal important patterns, but even a few days can bring insight. Use the next four pages to start this process with kindness toward yourself. When you feel ready, you can move on to the Trigger Management Plan to create a personal response strategy.

Trigger (What happened?)

_____
_____
_____
_____

Where were you?

_____
_____
_____

What happened right before?

_____
_____
_____

How did your body and emotions respond?

_____
_____
_____

Rate the intensity (1–10)

_____

Trigger (What happened?)

_____
_____
_____
_____

Where were you?

_____
_____
_____
_____

What happened right before?

_____
_____
_____
_____

How did your body and emotions respond?

_____
_____
_____
_____

Rate the intensity (1–10)

_____

Trigger (What happened?)

_____
_____
_____
_____

Where were you?

_____
_____
_____
_____

What happened right before?

_____
_____
_____
_____

How did your body and emotions respond?

_____
_____
_____
_____

Rate the intensity (1–10)

_____

Trigger (What happened?)

_____
_____
_____
_____
_____

Where were you?

_____
_____
_____
_____
_____

What happened right before?

_____
_____
_____
_____
_____

How did your body and emotions respond?

_____
_____
_____
_____
_____

Rate the intensity (1–10)

_____

Creating Your Trigger Management Plan

This section combines the essential elements of your Trigger Management Plan into one simple, easy-to-use tool. Keep it close whenever you feel overwhelmed or need a gentle way to restore your emotional balance.

Step 1. Triggers

What situations, words, or experiences activate your nervous system? *(Refer to your logs and list up to three.)*

1. _____
2. _____
3. _____

Step 2. Early Warning Signs

What physical or emotional signs tell you stress is building? *(Examples: shallow breath, muscle tension, irritability)*

_____
_____
_____
_____
_____
_____
_____
_____
_____
_____
_____

Step 3. Response Strategies

What action can you take at each intensity level?

Mild (1–3): 5 slow breaths, step outside for air
Moderate (4–6): text a friend, grounding object
Severe (7–10): call therapist, leave the situation

My Response Strategy

MILD	MODERATE	SEVERE

Step 4. Support System

Who/what can I reach for when triggered?
(Include people and tools, like grounding techniques or calming objects)

1. _____
2. _____
3. _____

Step 5. Safety Protocol

In case of a severe trigger, here's my safety plan:

Go to:
_____
_____

Call or text:
_____
_____

Say to myself:
_____
_____

Ask for:
_____
_____
_____
_____

"Having this plan ready helps me feel safer and more in control when I need it most"

Chapter 7
Fostering Connections and Community

How has your social life changed since your narcissistic relationship?
Reflect on the changes in your connections, relationships, and support systems.

What kind of community do you need most right now:
online, offline, or both?
*Take some time to explore and list at least three communities,
groups, or online spaces that feel like a good fit for you.*

_____
_____
_____
_____
_____
_____
_____
_____
_____
_____
_____
_____
_____

What types of support nurture you the most? Is it listening,
advice, shared activities, encouragement, or something else?
*Write down small steps you can take to incorporate more of that
into your life.*

_____
_____
_____
_____
_____
_____
_____
_____
_____
_____

How can I tell the difference between helpful sharing and oversharing?

_____
_____
_____
_____
_____
_____
_____
_____
_____

What feelings or signs help me recognize when I need to pause or protect myself?

_____
_____
_____
_____
_____
_____
_____
_____
_____

What old patterns do I notice in how I interact with groups or new people?

_____
_____
_____
_____
_____
_____
_____
_____
_____
_____
_____

How might these patterns be impacting my current relationships?

_____
_____
_____
_____
_____
_____
_____
_____
_____
_____

Who could I ask to mentor me, or who might I consider mentoring in the future?

_____
_____
_____
_____
_____
_____
_____
_____
_____
_____

How can I offer support to others in a way that nourishes me and doesn't deplete my energy?

_____
_____
_____
_____
_____
_____
_____
_____
_____
_____

How do I know when it's time to step back and rest from social connections?
What signs does my body or mind give me?

My Personal Connection Map

Draw a diagram of your current support system:

Inner Circle: People you trust completely
Middle Circle: People you're getting to know or rebuilding trust with
Outer Circle: Community spaces, online groups, or acquaintances

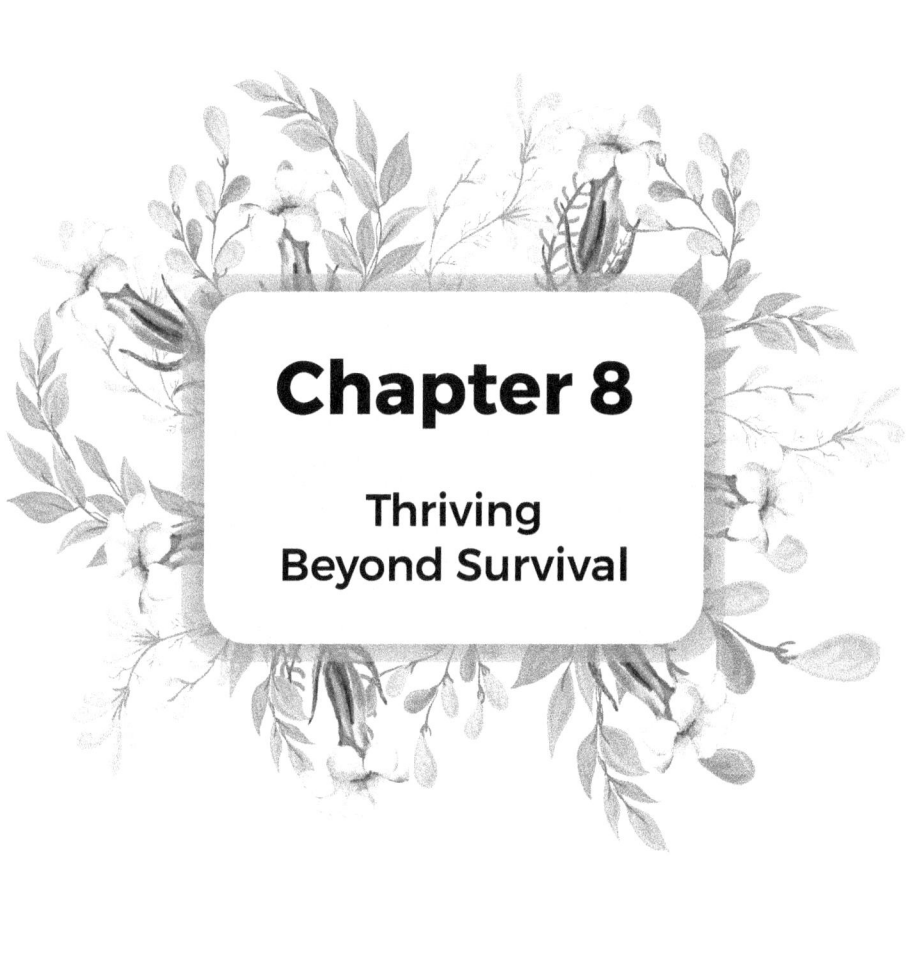

Chapter 8

Thriving Beyond Survival

Reflect on the moments when you feel most like yourself. Use these prompts to clarify your core values:

When do I feel most alive and true to myself?

_____
_____
_____
_____
_____
_____
_____
_____
_____
_____

What makes me feel proud of my choices?

_____
_____
_____
_____
_____
_____
_____
_____
_____
_____

What situations make me feel uncomfortable or wrong?

What do I want people to remember about me?

What would I stand up for, even if I stood alone?

When did I last feel deeply satisfied versus times I felt ashamed?

What parts of myself have I recently rediscovered or reclaimed? Describe how this feels.

Write a letter to your future self about what thriving looks like. Include your hopes, intentions, and reminders for the journey ahead.

Defining Personal Success

How do I define success for myself now?

Creating Your Personal Success Statement

Craft a personal success statement that reflects the person you are becoming and the life you want to lead. Use the prompts below to guide your words and vision.

"I am someone who…" (Describe who you are becoming.)

_____

_____

"I wake up each day feeling…" (Identify how you want to feel regularly.)

_____

_____

"In my relationships, I…" (Describe how you show up for others and how you expect to be treated.)

_____

_____

"Success, to me, means…" (Define success in your own words.)

_____

_____

Rewrite your full Personal Success Statement:

_____

_____

_____

_____

_____

_____

What specific actions, habits, or daily choices I can make this week that supports my Personal Success Statement?

___

Keep your Personal Success Statement somewhere you can see it every day, on your phone, tablet, or printed and posted on your fridge or mirror. Read it daily as a reminder of who you are becoming and the success you are creating.

SMART Goals

Use the SMART framework (Specific, Measurable, Achievable, Relevant, Time-bound) to create life goals that support your healing and growth.

Consider setting goals in these areas:

Personal Growth

_____
_____
_____

Relationships

_____
_____
_____

Health and Well-Being

_____
_____
_____

What is one playful or adventurous goal I can set that isn't about productivity or achievement, but simply about joy or curiosity?

Examples: Swim with the dolphins, go on a hot air balloon ride, have a picnic under the stars, learn to ice-skate, go on solo travel.

_____
_____
_____
_____

Freedom Inventory

Freedom is personal and evolves over time.
What does freedom mean to me today?

_____
_____
_____
_____
_____
_____
_____
_____
_____
_____
_____
_____
_____
_____
_____
_____
_____
_____
_____
_____
_____
_____
_____
_____
_____
_____
_____
_____
_____
_____

Look back at what you wrote about freedom. What feels missing in your life right now?
Make a list of five things you're ready to start today that will help you move closer to that freedom.

"I commit to at least one of these this week as a reminder of my personal freedom and joy."

What choices am I making now because I want to, not because I have to?

When do I feel most independent, and when do I still notice old patterns holding me back?

What is one area of my life where I'm ready to give myself more permission to choose freely, without guilt?

Living Out Loud

Living out loud means embracing your authenticity.
What are three things I will do this week to "live out loud"?

_____

"Each small goal you set, each boundary you maintain, each moment you choose yourself adds up to something powerful: a life lived on your own terms, in your full voice, without apology or permission."

What does it look like for me to be unapologetically myself today?

_____
_____
_____
_____
_____
_____
_____
_____
_____
_____
_____
_____

Where in my life do I still play small or hide my true self? How can I gently shift that?

_____
_____
_____
_____
_____
_____
_____
_____
_____
_____
_____
_____

What would it feel like to fully take up space in my own life? *Describe the sensations, actions, and thoughts that come with this reflection.*

Which parts of my story feel safe to share right now?
Write down a few stories or experiences you'd feel comfortable sharing in a group or with someone you trust.

_____
_____
_____
_____
_____
_____
_____
_____
_____
_____
_____
_____
_____
_____
_____
_____
_____
_____
_____
_____
_____
_____
_____
_____
_____
_____
_____
_____
_____

Accepting Feedback

How do I typically react to feedback or criticism? What physical sensations or emotions arise in my body?

_____
_____
_____
_____
_____
_____
_____
_____
_____
_____
_____
_____
_____
_____
_____
_____
_____
_____
_____
_____
_____
_____
_____
_____
_____
_____
_____

How can I distinguish between feedback that is truly helpful and feedback that feels manipulative or harmful?

What clarifying questions can I ask when I receive feedback to make sure it's constructive and supportive?

What milestone am I celebrating today?

What simple ritual can I use to celebrate my growth?
Spending a quiet day at the beach, booking a spa treatment, lighting my favorite incense, or treating myself to my favorite latte without guilt?

_____
_____
_____
_____
_____
_____
_____
_____
_____
_____
_____
_____

What's something I once denied myself that I now give myself permission to enjoy?

_____
_____
_____
_____
_____
_____
_____
_____
_____
_____
_____
_____

What's one small way I can celebrate the end of my week?
Watching a favorite old movie with popcorn, treating myself to takeout I love, or curling up with music and a cozy blanket?

Affirmation to Close This Chapter

This is your moment to pause and honor yourself. Every step, every boundary, every truth you've embraced has brought you here. Now it's time to celebrate not just surviving, but becoming.

Choose something that makes you feel alive, whether it's dancing in your living room, buying that dress you've always loved, or saying yes to a new adventure. Write it here, and let it become an affirmation of the life you're creating.

_____
_____
_____
_____
_____
_____
_____
_____
_____
_____
_____
_____
_____
_____
_____
_____
_____

"Your future is a blank canvas.
Live out loud and paint it in your own colors."

Final Thoughts and Resources

As you close this journal, pause to honor the journey you've taken. Every word you've written, every truth you've faced, is a testament to your courage. Healing is not a finish line, it's an unfolding path that moves at your own pace and in your own way.

You are worthy of love, peace, and joy. Continue to nurture yourself with patience and kindness as you grow.

If you feel called to go deeper or seek personalized guidance, I invite you to connect with me at
support@energiamindfulness.com
or visit **www.energiamindfulness.com** for additional support and resources.

Thank you for allowing this journal to walk with you. Remember: you are not alone, and your story matters.

With love,
Autumn

Share Your Voice

If this journal supported you in your healing journey, I would be deeply grateful if you left a review. Your words help others who are searching for support and hope to find this resource. Even a few sentences about your experience can help someone else feel less alone and more empowered to begin their own journey.

Thank you for sharing your voice, it matters more than you know.

www.ingramcontent.com/pod-product-compliance
Lightning Source LLC
Chambersburg PA
CBHW052130030426
42337CB00028B/5100